# 1 MONTH OF
# FREE
# READING

## at

## www.ForgottenBooks.com

By purchasing this book you are eligible for one month membership to ForgottenBooks.com, giving you unlimited access to our entire collection of over 1,000,000 titles via our web site and mobile apps.

To claim your free month visit:

www.forgottenbooks.com/free797312

ISBN 978-0-483-96390-0
PIBN 10797312

# PREFACE.

That vice ought to meet with reprobation, virtue with esteem, is a maxim
that emanates from the moral principle
on which all social union is founded.
No one will be sceptical enough to deny
a truth so obvious. Yet I fear there
will be many, so biassed by their passions ;—a sort of malignant drones, who
have not only ceased *laudanda facere,*
*sed etiam laudare ;*—a species of spider-
pated animals, who can suck *venom* out

of *medicinal* flowers,—as to call in question the *expediency* of reducing this salutary maxim into practice, and to regard, therefore, these ingenuous Sketches with an unfriendly eye. If any such there should be, and with no great portion of second sight I am almost confident there will, I would humbly beseech them to listen to what the pilot of the little bark has to say in his own behalf; and perhaps he may be able to convince these testy folks, that he is not acting *contra bonos mores* in his present fishing excursion, undertaken purely from motives of amity and good will.

It is certainly the *duty* of every man, as a being who looks beyond the limits of this narrow existence, who trusts for future happiness upon his share of present perfection, to use and encourage every mean that may tend to improve and exalt his character. It will as readily be granted, that the path to excellence is deceitful and difficult. There is no individual, however perfect his intellectual constitution, who is not apt to mistake the road, if he trusts entirely to *his own judgment ;* for self-love is ever on the alert to mislead. Hence it is a common observation, that men never form so good a judgment of their own actions, as of those of their neighbours. It is certainly desirable, that this selfish bias should be counteracted : And every man ought to feel grateful to any friendly observer, who, with polite freedom, points out his errors, and shews him again into the path of rectitude. What can be more convenient and useful to the one, more generous and disinterested in the other? Would we not reprobate any traveller in a strange country, who, without a chart or even

a signpost to direct him, should, from
a silly vanity of his own judgment,
continue his way without making any
inquiry at those he met, whether or
not he was following the proper course?
The character of any man's understanding, is certainly as much implicated ;
who, professing to pursue that excel-
ence which his duty points out, trusts
entirely to his own opinion of his conduct, and will not lend an ear to the advice of others.

It is true, that this ability in one individual, to discover the faults of another,
is the consequence of this very self-love,
which tends to render men so errant and
unsteady.

> None, none descends into himself to find
> The secret imperfections of his mind,
> But every one is eagle-eyed to see
> Another's fault, and his deformity.

But, though originating from a bad source, no one ought to entertain less respect for a quality which is avowedly useful in its consequences. He ought to remember, that good frequently proceeds from evil; and if he can derive any benefit from his neighbour's frailties, he should forget the source of it, and be grateful *ab imo pectore.*

It is usual to maintain, that as personal observations are apt to degenerate into *scandal,* all such observations ought to be suppressed. No man entertains a greater abhorrence of scandal than I do. I detest it as one of the greatest evils that can invade society. I regret that it should ever have imposed its hydra form on the beneficial and dignified power of criticism. But that a right has been abused is no rea-

son that it should be discontinued. If
its genuine tendency is salutary, we
should endeavour to lop off the spurious
.branches, to restore it to its primitive
tone, and *then* it ought to be encouraged
in its operation.

If in this innocent lucubration, therefore, I shall be found to have adhered
to the legitimate use of criticism,—the
detection of *error*, and the disclosure of
*truth*,—I rest for approbation on the basis
of justice and utility. If in any thing I
have deviated from fact, I trust it will
be attributed to misapprehension and
not to wilfulness; that it will be regarded
with friendly lenity, and not with acri-
monious severity. I am too sensible of
the fallibility of human judgment to
think I may not have erred; but a know-

ledge of my heart entitles me to claim the merit of good intentions.

One thing I may add, as entitled to no small consideration. However little *good* these sketches may do among my fellow-citizens, they can do *no harm*. They are calculated to do wrong to no one.

————— " If they do him right,
" Then he hath wronged himself. If he be free,
" Why, then, my taxing like a wild goose flies,
" Unclaimed of any man."

It is not improper to remind my readers, that the *application* of these sketches lies with them, and not with me. I pledge them, therefore, in their hands, with the hope that they will avoid any erroneous comments or interpretations, which may implicate individuals whom the author had not in view, and to whom they do not apply;

so that none may be injured, or have ground for resentment.

" I am the father of each child 'tis true,
" But every babe its christ'ning owes to you."

# CHARACTERS

## OF A

# GREAT TOWN.

---

## LORD ANTICOUGH.

---

*Asinus quanquam Tyrio conspectus in ostro*
*Semper erit tardus.*

BUCHANAN.

*Adorn an ass in robes, with all your pains,*
*Dull, stupid, spiritless, he still remains.*

---

PRECEDENCE is a tribute due to distinction, although distinction is not always founded on superiority of merit. The reverence of wealth or dignity
is the effect of an artificial state of society, and the
observance of which a regard to society demands.
*Pay tribute to whom tribute is due, honour to whom*

A

*honour*, is the expressive maxim of the Sacred Wri‑
tings : So likewise our immortal Bard,

———— *Respect great place ! and let the devil*
*Be sometimes honour'd for his burning throne.*

MEASURE FOR MEASURE.

The force of these maxims, however, a churlish
world has always been unwilling to acknowledge.
But of the general failing I am proud to disown a
share, and to hold them forth as my motive for
selecting Lord ANTICOUGH from the crowd of ob‑
jects that press around me, as entitled to primary
consideration.  I select him, not as preeminent in
singularity ; I pay regard to the *blushing honours* of
his Lordship.

The world is generally slow in forming an opi‑
nion of any individual character ; but, when an opi‑
nion is once formed, it is usually decisive.  My
Lord Anticough has been a considerable time in
the field of public employment, and the estimation
of his fellow-citizens may now be considered as well
ripened.  I regret it falls not to my lot to congra‑
tulate his Lordship with the meed of applause,
The public opinion of his character has taken au

unfavourable bias. He is quaintly termed " *A Common Man*," which, in the language of society, imports one neither eminent in virtue nor in vice; whose qualities are of the plainest cast; who proceeds through life without leaving any trace of his progress; and of whom nothing more will be said when he dies, than has been expressively said of another:

" *Colas vivoit, Colas est mort.*"

It is the general complaint, that the spurious importance attached to wealth, has raised his Lordship to a dignity for which his abilities are inadequate. How can one, it is asked, raised from a low condition in life, and destitute of education, properly comprehend or execute the duties of a trust so important? Ignorant of the true principles of political economy, has he been able to act with propriety or firmness? Has he not been carried away by his own ignorance, by popular clamour, or by intrigue and sophistry, to pursue measures pernicious to the interests of the community; or to adopt others utterly abortive and useless? Unacquainted with moral science, has he been able to avoid many moral deliquencies, which the laws do not hold forth to reprobation? Has he not neglected the moral government of those whose conduct comes under his control? Devoid of all acquaintance with the philosophy of the mind and a rational theology, has he not been often induced to join the cry of prejudice, to act with all the illiberality of party-spirit, perhaps to resign his conduct to the guidance of superstition?

It may be said, these queries embrace extreme conclusions; and that, allowing much of the defects alleged, Lord Anticough may nevertheless fill his situation, not entirely without credit to himself, and advantage to the community. Is it necessary that every ruler should be a LYCURGUS? Must they all be men of great and speculative minds? Idle fanfaronade of excellence, which can seldom be realised! Is not the plain honest sobriety of his Lordship's character the surest pledge of an easy and temperate administration? A sober man will be diffident; he will be considerate; he will not hazard any deviation from old and established systems, but follow the path which has been beaten before him; he will be fearful of offence, and cooperate in all the feelings and wishes of the people; he will avoid all manner of transgression against popular opinion. And has not such a line of conduct a well-founded claim to our regard and esteem ?

This cautious timidity may indeed protect him from the blame of transgression, or at least tend to palliate his errors. But, in avoiding Scylla, the mariner is taught to beware of Charybdis : And what is all government but a troubled sea, beset with rocks and quicksands ; with storms and whirlwinds? It is not enough that a ruler avoid the rock of transgression; he must not fall into the error of omission. The one sin is not less heinous than the other. Ignorance in private life may be deemed a venial fault; those errors which result from it may pass without censure, if they appear free from evil. But in public situations of trust, in extraordinary employments, the world have a right to look for adequate talents. The actions of public functionaries are designed always to do benefit ; if they do not, they cannot be justified. They do hurt, unless they do good ; they are scandalous, if they are suspicious. Their popularity cannot save them from reprehension. The people are least of all judges of what is beneficial for them, and it is the object of raising a few into authority over the rest, that talent and wisdom may decide. Philosophy is the only source of right government.

"*All policy but her's is false and rotten.*"

There is no ground, however, to lament Lord An-ticough's preeminence; every murmur ought to be quashed. Let it be remembered that fools as well as wise men must have their day; that the one class has an influence in society, as well as the other, which enforces the unfortunate necessity of keeping on mutual good terms, that each may jog on its way in comfort. That " all men are born equal, and continue equal in their rights," was the celebrated maxim of the French politicians. The evil may be great, but it is irremediable; and society must sub-mit to many periods of weak and foolish administra-tion, to enjoy the return of energy and wisdom. It is an evil, too, which may have its good effects; for contrast enables mankind to discriminate more clear-ly between good and evil, more steadily to prize the one, and detest the other.

From the consideration of my Lord Anticough's public character, let me take a glance at his pri-vate life. Here I survey a more fiery field. Nothing is found to respect,—a great deal to detest. It has been remarked by some divine, that men are always disposed to sin, when they can do so with *safety*. The remark is strong, but expresses much truth. The fear of public obloquy has prevented many a man from being a villain; the love of public esteem has directed many a bad heart to the worthiest pursuits. Who would suspect that my Lord Anticough, so calm and equal in public life, is the victim of violent passions in private? A more haughty or imperious master than his Lordship, a stronger instance of conjugal subjection, than his *cara sposa*, does not perhaps tread the earth from Indus to the Pole. The gratification of this worshipful dignitary is the *primum mobile* of his domestic economy, and the ease and comfort of every other being is sacrificed to it. To indulge a lofty serenity, is his Lordship's foible; and to such a height does he carry this important whim, that the slapping of a door, or the escape of a cough, is sure to disorder his whole system, and to bring on the unhappy cause a torrent of invective. How weak, how despicable, must such conduct appear, to every kind and temperate head of a family! Public and private tyrants are equally detestable, and the good and the virtuous must always rejoice, when the former meet with a Brutus;—the latter, with a Censor.

# DR WORMWOOD.

---

——————————— *The world's large tongue*
*Proclaims you for a man replete with mocks,*
*Full of comparisons and wounding flouts,*
*Which you on all estates will execute,*
*That lie within the mercy of your wit.*
SHAKESPEARE.

---

IT has often been maintained, that literary pursuits have a *salutary* influence upon the conduct of an individual in common life. They are said to soften the temper; to cherish those delicate emotions in which true virtue consists; and, by expanding our views of human nature, to mortify the passions of interest and ambition, and, at the same time, to give us a greater sensibility of all the decencies and duties of life. Cicero emphatically terms the votaries of the arts and sciences, heroes of peace. But experience, I think, does not support the assertion, and evinces, in general, that the frailty of nature is rather nourished than subdued by philosophical acquirements. There seems a steady propensity in the constitution of man towards imperfection ; to none more than that of self-love,-than which, there is not a richer source of illiberal and unsocial qualities. And it will be allowed, that this failing has never been more common nor more powerful than in those whom the world has termed *philosophers*. It would seem, that in proportion as the extent of their knowledge raised them in the scale of intelligence above the herd of mankind, so their love of themselves, and their contempt of others increased ; that instead of being more impressed with the various decencies and duties of that social part for which man has been designed by Providence, they have not only imbibed the most thorough disregard of them, but appear to have deemed it a degradation to mingle in the sphere of common enjoyment. They have become coarse, illiberal, and unmannerly. The gratification of their self-love, and all the wild passions which it stirred up, has been their ruling motive of action. Diogenes, and not Plato, has formed the model of their conduct.

Some of the brightest ornaments in the circle of

literature afford examples of these remarks. The spleen of Swift, the vanity of Pope, and the rude illiberality of Johnson, savoured little of the enlightened philosophy of their minds. A humorous catalogue, says one of these great men himself, might be formed of " the fears of the brave, and the follies of " the wise." What a wide distinction is there betwixt precept and practice ! How oft do individuals assume the right of catechizing their fellows, who stand themselves in need of tuition ! In the romance of life they are divinities ; in its history they are men : amid all their wisdom they still continue to be frail, more culpably so from their superior knowledge of what is right.

" *It lights a torch to show their shame the more.*"

Every age lengthens the list of " wise fools," and

" *Fame, which round the world delights to stray,*"

has caught the name of WORMWOOD.

Dr Wormwood's abilities and knowledge have deservedly acquired him a large share of professional reputation. Intimately acquainted with the various relations of the human constitution, and possessed of strong powers of judgment and discrimination, no man perhaps is better able to sift the prognosis of a case, and of course to apply its remedy. When our health or existence is in danger, we naturally court the most skilful aid. This is a situation in which we least of all are guided by our likes and dislikes. From this principle, the practice of Dr Wormwood is extensive, although upon every other, I am inclined to think, he would be doomed to neglect and obscurity.

> *All doors are barr'd against a bitter flout,*
> *Snarl still he may, but he must snarl without.*
>
> PERSIUS.

Wormwood presents none of that affability which every physician ought to possess in order to inspire confidence; none of that tenderness necessary to alleviate shame, or to countenance delicacy. Stern and sarcastic in his manners, he grates the feelings, always most tender in infirmity, and imposes silence on the tongue. His face appears to have made a perpetual divorce from smiles. He treats his patients rather as subjects for ridicule, than relief; indulges in impertinent and superfluous interrogatories; and is not always observant of that fidelity which ought to distinguish so confidential a character as a physician.

Fully sensible of his skill, he is not less careful that it shall have its price. The worthy Doctor cannot perhaps charge his conscience with the iniquity of one single *gratuitous* act;—unless where he had the view of gaining more by his generosity, than he could by his extortion. Humanity never troubles his breast; charity shuns it as " a dry and parched " land, in which there are no waters." His hands are always open,

" *Not to* bestow, *but to* receive."

Gold is the grand *sine qua non ;* it is the passport to all advice ; it is the key to the treasures of his mind. Oft has he been known to turn the poor wretch, pining under the double burden of sickness and want, from his door, without affording, not pecuniary assistance, but the small tribute of *advice,* which was earnestly implored ! Humanity shudders at an act of so much cruelty, shrinks from an object of so deep depravity.

The love of money produces many singular changes and contortions on this worthy Doctor. He is not content with pursuing it by professional means, with confining himself to a traffic with Charon. The *garb* of Hippocrates is often thrown aside ; and we behold the Doctor enveloped in a *sowing sheet*, or loaded with invoices and plans. He farms, builds, exports : he dabbles in every thing by which he can make money, and, in the way of making a bargain, may defy rivalship.

Wormwood is a Cynic of a new cast. He despises and snarls at the world ; but places his happiness in the enjoyment of a profusion of earthly things. Yet he loves not wealth as a mean of acquiring some separate and solid benefit ; he loves it for its intrinsic worth, that vilest degradation of human appetite. He is not entirely an Elwes or a Sillerton, for he allows himself every kind of moderate indulgence : But he presents the meanness of both in his exorbitant thirst for lucre, and far exceeds them in the baseness of the means which he employs. We are disposed to *pity* a man who will not enjoy the favours which fortune has heaped upon him, but who husbands them for posterity : We *detest* one who endeavours to amass wealth by sucking the pockets of his neighbours, by imposing a tax on wretchedness and misery.

The desires of Wormwood present a singular contrast to those of Shakespeare's Cynic; and by modifying a little the prayer of Timon, we may behold the Doctor breathing in spirit and in truth.

> Immortal Gods, bestow some pelf.
> I pray for no man but myself.
> Grant I may never prove so fond,
> To trust man on his word or bond;
> Nor yet a beggar for his weeping;
> Nor e'er believe one dead who's sleeping[*];
> Nor patient treat with my advice,
> Unless he first pay down the price.
>
> ———————
>
> Amen! Amen! Ye Gods so be it,
> Let all men *ail*, if I but *fee* it.

———————

[*] It is related, not of Dr Wormwood, but of one to whom he bears no little resemblance, that a wealthy citizen who had the misfortune to require his visits, was in the custom of having the gold always ready in his hand to electrify the Doctor when he felt his pulse. One day it happened, on the Doctor's making his stated call, that the servant

With all these blemishes in his character, Wormwood is a man who has drank deeply from the
streams of literature; whose fame, for varied and extensive knowledge, for ingenious and able disquisition, is spread far and wide. But where is the *salutary* influence of literary habits on *his* conduct? Have
they expanded and softened his mind? Have they
raised him above all selfish considerations? Have
they warmed his breast with benevolence? Have
they impressed a *superior* observance of any of the
social duties upon him?

*O curæ hominum, o quantum est in rebus inane !*

---

informed him " *All was over.*" " Over!" re-echoed
the Doctor, as the remembrance of the customary
fee flashed on his mind, " Impossible! he cannot
be dead yet. No! No! Let *me* see him,—some
trance or heavy sleep perhaps." The Doctor was
introduced into the sable apartment; he took the
hand of the pale corpse, applied his finger to that
artery which once ebbed with life, gave a sorrowful
shake of his head, while with a trifling *legerdemain*
he relieved from the grasp of death *two guineas,*
which in truth had been destined for him. " Aye,
Aye, good folks," said the Doctor, " he is dead;
there is a *destiny in all things ;*" and full of his
shrewd sagacity, turned upon his heel.

# DR TRANSIT.

*There are whom heaven has blest with store of wit,*
*Yet want as much again to govern it.*

Pope.

Were it in the power of the pen to produce the effects of the painter's pencil, and to pourtray the character of the mind as expressed in the features of the face, I would represent to my readers a young man, high indeed in the estimation of the world, but far higher in his own opinion. I would paint the expression of inward satisfaction sparkling in his eyes, and frowning from his brow, in the proud gravity of assumed self-consequence. I would depict contempt in his looks, as he sur-

B

veys around him men whom heaven has not blest
with *his* talents, nor with *his* education; whose
merit it has been to pass through life with the approbation of the few, and far removed from the
laughter of the many; whose source of happiness
was their honest and well-spent life, and not the silly admiration of the ignorant, or the yet emptier
bubble of self-importance.

——————————————— " *Hæc est*
" *Vita solutorum misera ambitione.*"

" *Such is the life from bad ambition free.*"

The world will exclaim, " *This is* Dr TRANSIT,"
but very probably the Doctor will deny the likeness,
and discover it in his friend; for, of all prejudices,
that in favour of one's self is the blindest, and most
difficult to be cured:

" *It travels through, nor quits us when we die;*"

—a quality in the composition of every man, which,
as it is governed and directed, may incite to the

noblest efforts, or cover with lasting ridicule. In the rich soil of the Doctor's mind, nourished as it was by his habits and pursuits, it flourished luxuriantly, and has become the ruling passion of his soul.

Believing he knows as much as any man, he has the air of being perfectly satisfied on that head, and of envying nobody; but, aspiring beyond the limits of reputation to which this terrestrial system confines him, he now seeks to elevate his fame to immortality, by the discovery of new firmaments and new worlds, conceived in the wildness of his imagination only, but already embodied by the vigour of hope.

This knowledge of astronomy, as it enlarges our conceptions of the Great Author of this, and every other system of being, is the most proper, likewise, according to Fontenelle, to teach humility to a just and right formed mind, from a contemplation of the immensity of the universe, and the consequent insignificance of man in the vast scale of existence. In Dr Transit, however, it increases only that low ambition which has not for its object to render us better and wiser, but to obtain public notice; and that silly vanity which is gratified by public admiration.

The language of Transit forcibly discovers the feelings of his mind. In the proud tone of conscious superiority, he intrudes on every company; he pesters the learned, and insults the ignorant, with impertinent recitals of his abilities, his merits, and his labours. " Did you hear my lecture last night?" he exclaims. " Did you not feel astonished? Was it not great? comprehensive! wonderful! Why, Sir, I think my labours are immense! I think I do more, Sir, in one day, than all the College of Doctors in a twelvemonth!"—Strange effect of science! that a man, as he grows more learned, should grow likewise more impertinent and ridiculous; and, as he excels in merit, that he should be more hated and despised in society!

Yet I have seen Dr Transit affect a modest air; for he has been told that modesty becomes a great man; as people of a short size crouch on entering a room for fear of striking their heads.

The just tribute of applause ought not, however, to be withheld from merit: and I am willing to allow that Dr Transit possesses *some* sense, *some* abilities, and *some* learning ; but

*Apparent rari nantes in gurgite vasto.*

VIRGIL.

# MRS D. PELZIER.

——————— *O che gentile*
*Scongiuro ha ritrovato questo sciocco*
*Di rammentarmi la mia giovenezza,*
*Il ben passato e la presente noia.*

TASSO.

*A pleasant way the rogue has tu'en,*
*Back to recall my youth, and show*
*What once I was, and what I am.*

I T is with pleasure I turn from the vices and follies of the one sex, to trace the lighter, more delicate, but more capricious peculiarities of the other.
I may say *capricious,* since Lord Chesterfield has
said before me, that he never knew a woman in all
his life act consistently for an hour together. The
term may be easily forgiven, therefore; and the more
willingly too, as I do not extend the authority so

far, nor put it to so bad an use, as I might, in the present case. I might relate, for instance, many a pleasant story of caprice in Mrs PELZIER, even after she had become a wife, but long before she had learned *to wear a cap ;* and entertain the reader, on sufficient grounds of truth, with curious dialogues between the lady and her husband about the necessity of wearing caps at all, or the pleasures of a rocking horse. But these are trifles that may be related of every young lady, of young English ladies in particular: And I disdain such little methods of painting a character, which, it would appear from using them, I was unable to distinguish otherwise. Let me endeavour to catch those greater lineaments which mark and particularize the individual in the circle in which she moves.

In societies, as in governments, there are always a few who appear to be destined by their talents, their situations, and by circumstances, to lead and direct the mass of the people ; to influence them, at least, on the side of virtue, or to be their guides in the paths of vice and folly.. Whichever part they act, the effect is never indifferent. Their example spreads to all around them, and descends even to the lowest.

Mrs Pelzier acquired this preeminence in the community to which she belongs, at an early age. This was a period of pleasure and gaiety, of splendour and extravagance; but her cultivated mind, and the elegance of her taste, refined the former, and concealed the evil of the latter. Under this alluring disguise, her *bourgeoise* neighbours were little able to discover the poison, and drank the chalice off to the lowest dregs. She was caressed, envied, and followed; and her faults became copies for the conduct of those who imagined that profusion and finery were elegance, while they wanted that taste which refined the extravagance of Mrs Pelzier. They grew fond of the course of folly into which they had slipped, and continued their career with eagerness. Extravagance excited a spirit of emulation; and emulation, in return, inflamed the madness of extravagance.

> " *As the small pebble stirs the peaceful lake,*
> " *The centre mov'd, a circle strait succeeds,*
> " *Another still, and still another spreads,*"

so did this spirit extend among the fair inhabitants of the city. But in this splendour they appeared like those who have recourse to ornament to conceal their ugliness : their defects were not only undisguised, but others were produced ; the tawdriness of the whole was heightened, and its vanity made more absurd. They raised themselves, to speak in the Italian manner, to the height of ridicule, and sunk their husbands, many of them, in the depths of bankruptcy.

That these have been the consequences of this dangerous spirit, none, I believe, will presume to deny. But it would be unjust to attribute them entirely to the influence of Mrs Pelzier, and to make her the author of every folly that was committed in the circle of fashion during her reign. I do believe there would have been folly enough in the circle had she never presided over it, though there might not possibly have been so much extravagance. But it serves to show how much depends on the conduct of those who have attained an eminence in society ; how nice the line is, that divides the affluence of rank from extravagance ; and how much it is necessary (it is de Vega who makes the remark, I think) in those who lead and direct the spirit of the society they form a part of, to lead and direct it to just and proper ends :
" Quanto es necesario in ellos quienes guian y diri-

" gen el genio de la sociedad endonde estan, diri-
" girlo a los objetos justos y propios."

Mrs Pelzier is now in the wane, and her claims
to admiration have long since ceased to be acknow-
ledged. She must now found her power, if she
would preserve it, and there is little difficulty of preserving it against those who tread at present the
mazes of fashion, on the basis of esteem, and leave
the youthful to dazzle and to be flattered.

" *So when the sun's broad beam has tired the sight,*
" *All mild ascends the moon's more sober light;*
" *Serene in virgin modesty she shines,*
" *And unobserved the glaring orb declines.*"

# COUNSELLOR VELLUM.

---

*Our city's institutions, and the terms*
*Of common justice, y'are as pregnant in*
*As art and practice hath enriched any*
*That we remember.*

SHAKESPEARE.

---

THE power of habit, either to strengthen or coun-
teract the natural dispositions of men, is almost unlimited. The chords of the heart are of a pliant nature, and fall readily under the impression of exterior circumstances. When once impelled from their
natural bias, a rapid assimilation to the change
takes place, while the tide of life continues to flow
with undiminished energy. So the tender scion,
transplanted from the open field to the garden-wall,
abandons its natural propensities, and, under the

shackles of art, spreads luxuriantly forth in grotesque and unnatural directions.

This influence of habit is strongly marked in the character of the individual before me. In the dawn of life, while nature continued to give the spring to action, few were more distinguished for their amiable qualities than VELLUM.—Sincere and tender in his attachments, polished and engaging in his manners, he was an object of general attraction. But, induced by *the necessity* of following a respectable and lucrative profession, rather than from any relish towards legal practice, he threw himself into the fast arms of the law, and from its hard bosom has since imbibed nothing but selfishness and distrust.

His industry was now exerted to obtain a subsistence through the quarrels and animosities of his fellow-creatures, and his heart soon became poisoned by the deceit, injustice, and knavery amid which it was his lot to labour. He imbibed a degree of cunning into his own conduct, and became distrustful of that of others. His sentiments lost their pristine complexion, and became clouded and selfish. A view to his own interest assumed the rule of all his actions ; he became estranged from every finer relation which softens and adorns the path of life :

> *Vers'd in the commerce of deceit*
> *How soon the heart forgets to beat !*
> *The blood runs cold, at interest's call*
> *We look with equal eyes on all.*
>
> \* \* \* \* \* \* \* \* \* \*
> \* \* \* \* \* \* \* \* \* \*
>
> *Affection dies, a vernal flower,*
> *And love the blossom of an hour.*
>
> *Then lovely nature is expell'd,*
> *And friendship is romantic held ;*
> *Then prudence comes, with hundred eyes,*
> *The veil is rent, the vision flies !*
>
> LOGAN.

Convenience has assumed the place of principle, and thrown its flimsy mantle over the mind of Vellum. He maintains a wide society, because to keep company is genteel, and a portion of time is thus agreeably dissipated. But amid the flattering crowd who call themselves his friends, he knows not the delight of one solid attachment. The companionable qualities of hard drinking and sober conversation, form the brittle chain of connection.—The Counsellor is of an amorous disposition, but of too cool and sensible a turn of mind to assume the airs of a general gallant. His passion is purely of a sensual nature, and its gratification a matter of shillings and pence.

Although Vellum's habits have sunk him in the scale of worth, he is not altogether an unuseful member of society. He is eminent in his profession for ability, and I may add integrity. He is not what we would strictly call an *honest* lawyer, one who weighs the cause more than the fee, who would rather be dumb than plead for injustice. A being of this sort is a rarity in the legal circle, who would stir up enemies in it as readily as quills may be raised on the fretful porcupine. Vellum's practice is as much in the offensive as defensive ; his skill is as often employed in out-baffling as in supporting right.

" *Bid virtue crouch, bid vice exalt her horn,*
" *Bid cowards thrive, put honesty to flight,*
" *Vellum will prove, or try to prove it right.*'

But this is all in the common way, and nobody blames him for it. He receives on every hand the credit of strict fidelity to the cause in which he engages, and will not, Janus-faced, take a retaining fee from the plaintiff, and afterwards a sinister bribe from the defendant. He is zealous in his client's cause: He does not follow its course through the courts, but manages it : He has a perfect knowledge of his profession, and, with a large share of penetration and sagacity, proves an excellent anatomist of *meum* and *tuum.*

He partakes of an accusation common to his brethren, that of being exorbitant in his charges : but this is the language of a foul-mouthed rabble, not of men of sense. A lawyer's profession is considered too much as mercenary : the money given him is a just acknowledgment for his advice and well-intended endeavours ; and if the object of contention should vanish, perhaps, in the abyss of proceedings, the blame ought oftener to be laid on the intricacy of the case, or the forms of court, than to the improper conduct of the individual who managed the contest.

I may add another observation. Vellum is not what a French author describes a lawyer to be, the dread and terror of his neighbours. He suffers them to live in quiet, without continual alarms of actions and indictments; nor does he make any piece of land fall nine years' purchase, because it lies within three leagues of him.

In fine, Vellum, though not an amiable, is not a very bad man; though sordid, he never passes the bounds of justice to obtain money; though a lawyer, he continues to observe the law.

*Mundus erit qui non offendet sordibus, atque*
*In utram partem cultus miser.*

HORACE.

# MR MACSAPLESS.

———————

————— *Uxorem, Posthume, ducis ?*
*Dic quâ Tisiphone, quibus exagitare colubris ?*
                                        JUV.

*A niggard, old like thee, to change his life !*
*What fury would possess thee with a wife ?*

———————

My Lord Bacon has said, in one of his essays, that " wives are young men's mistresses, companions for middle age, and old men's nurses ; yet that he was reputed one of the wise men who made answer to the question, when a man should marry, —' A young man not yet, an elder man not at all." The argument is here so ingeniously stated on both sides, and so conclusively for each, that every man may find reason enough to justify his conduct, however much he may deviate from reason or decency. Of those who venture on this important change,

c

no one perhaps becomes more ridiculous than he whom the necessity of a nurse does not urge to enter the pale of matrimony, but the delirium of a whim. It is men of this cast who fill up, in the scale of error, the distance that lies between the errors of folly and those of vice; who partake of both, and being thus more obnoxious, become more worthy of public censure.

The general reflection applies directly in the present instance. It is not the age of Mr MACSAPLESS we laugh at, when we see his decrepid form trembling over a staff, or sinking to the ground: we laugh only when we reflect that that cold withered body seeks to ape the heat and vigour of youth ; that those shrivelled arms hold, like a sepulchre, within them, a young and charming girl. Here, age carries with it no reverence ; it gains no respect: like a shade, it serves only to mark more strongly the features of folly in the picture ; but, unlike other pictures, where the eye is relieved, and the beauty of the whole is produced by the contrast, the mind is here shocked and disgusted, and the draught becomes an overcharged caricature.

I might extend the sketch, and exhibit Mr Macsapless at home, where his follies are much better known, and his weakness is much better felt, did I not fear to disgust the reader by a description of the frailties and absurdities of this poor dotard. Nor to the lady of the piece shall I say much. The world loudly proclaims she sacrificed willingly her youth and charms to her love of money. It may be so: from a motive, likewise, similar to that which Martial alleges in one of his epigrams:

" *To Sapless married ! what reason ?—Oh, enough,*
" *Sapless, you know, has got a churchyard cough."*

But whatever her reasons were, I forbear with pleasure to enlarge upon them. She merits our pity; she needs not surely our reproaches. Let us take leave of her in the words of Waller:

" *Since thou would'st needs, bewitch'd with some ill*
        " *charms,*
" *Be buried in these monumental arms,*
" *All we can wish is, May that earth lie light,*
" *Upon thy tender limbs ! and so goodnight."*

# MRS HALFWORTH.

*Show your poverty of spirit,*
*And in dress place all your merit ;*
*Give yourself ten thousand airs.*

SWIFT.

IT is a true observation, because founded on a knowledge of the human heart, that those who can lay no claim to high birth, affect in general to despise it, as an advantage unworthy their regard. There are others, however, who lay too much stress on this advantage, and run into the opposite extreme. These are they who have grown proud as they have grown wealthy, and fear the more, and the more justly, as they rise to rank and eminence, lest the lustre of their new honours should be sullied by any nice inquiry into the origin of their family. They assume, therefore, what the poorest and most common person of those they live among is able to deny them,—a pre-eminence of birth ; or else they endeavour, by some silly contrivance, to conceal in obscurity, or involve in uncertainty, the real source from which they spring. They remove, for example, the place of their birth to a great distance, and out of the immediate view of such as are willing to interest themselves about it; but are not willing, or are unable to trace it there, by the uncertain light which is afforded them of a few hints. Were these pages to fall into the hands of Mrs HALFWORTH, the lady whose character I sketch, she would no doubt feel readily, and fully too, the truth of all these observations ; and should I go on to explain more clearly what I have touched upon, and point out *England*, for instance, as a place extremely favourable for affording this obscurity and uncertainty, it might bring to her remembrance ————, but I stop,

———— *allor che in core hai ferma,*
*Gia la feral sentenza* ————

for I should be carried to make many strong allusions, and strong allusions might hurt the fair subject of this stricture.

I may proceed, however, to describe those features in the character of Mrs Halfworth, by the
delineation of which I shall not raise in her any
feeling of anger or pain, but rather a feeling that is
allied very nearly to *pleasure*. For there are women,
we know, whose vanity it is to be extravagant at
any expence,—at the expence even of virtue and fortune; and who are willing enough to flatter this vanity, by the sacrifice even of their character. I
mean not to say that Mrs Halfworth carries this
passion to so great a height; but I will be bold to
assert the lady would not feel angry, were she told
that she is the most extravagant woman in ————.

This sin of extravagance is a very grievous sin,
not only in itself, but also in its consequences,
both immediate and remote; not only as it affects
the extravagant themselves, but as it affects the age
they live in, and as it descends to posterity. It is
a spirit, which, when it enters a woman's head, drives
out immediately all prudence, moderation, decency,
and common sense; and when it descends to the
heart, impels her irresistibly to wage war upon all
such as are possessed with the same rage of spend-
ing. It creates thus many battles, skirmishes, and
affrays, in the shapes of rival dinner and supper par-

ties, balls, and new dresses, where those weapons called new plate, new china, new trinkets, new laces, and new silks, are levelled and darted by the combatants with great dexterity, rapidity, and fury, to the manifest destruction of the lady's health in the first place, and the husband's purse in the second; for in such battles, unlike all others, a victory is sure to exhaust more than a defeat. It incites them too, according to the constitution of their characters, and the temper of their vanity, to affect airs of haughtiness and dignity, that become them no better than if they once had moved in the lowest sphere of life; or else to assume little airs of softness and delicacy, which observers are ready to consider as mere affectation, arising from a very weak head, and a very vain heart.

As to posterity, it is obvious, that this profusion and riot, this aping of high-life, will soon swallow up the competence their labours may have gained them, and leave to their offspring that portion only with which they themselves perhaps began the world,—the portion of ignorance and poverty.

The terms I use sound harshly, but the censure is just, and it will appear to be so in the highest degree, and upon the highest reason, if we look around

among such as I have characterized. We shall see
how deeply this vice has taken root, and how far
it has spread, among the wives of our citizens : we
may not only deplore the evil, but we may do more :
we may employ for the correction of it such means
as it is in the power of every individual to use, towards the improvement or reformation of the society
to which he belongs; and, in fine, though these ends
are hardest to be obtained, when they are the most
necessary, yet the endeavours of every good man
ought therefore to be the more employed to obtain
them, that domestic virtue and happiness may be
the better preserved and secured. Should such a
spirit be raised to these purposes, in my fellow-citizens, I humbly beg leave to recommend Mrs
Halfworth to their early and special attention.

# REV. A. MASKWELL.

*Touch'd with each weakness which he does arraign,*
*With vanity he talks against the vain,*
*With ostentation does to meekness guide,*
*Proud of his periods levell'd against pride.*

ANON.

A CLERGYMAN who devotes his exertions to the amendment of his fellow-creatures, who enforces his precepts by their strict exemplification in his own practice, deservedly ranks high in worth and respectability. Such a character is not less good and useful than the opposite is vile and dangerous ;—one who admonishes with equal ability, but exhibits in his conduct the pattern of every vice which he holds forth to reprobation. His behaviour throws ridicule over his professions : the vicious laugh at his denunciations, despise him for his hypocrisy, and the well-inclined slip into vice from that impression of insincerity which they naturally imbibe from the example of their preceptor.

The popular talents of the individual before me raised him to an ecclesiastical charge, which is in fact *easy*, yet affords a trifling revenue to the incumbent. The " pomp of circumstance" had taken a strong hold of Maskwell's mind, and, with an indulged fondness for good living, made him view the narrowness of his means with a mixture of regret and spleen. His appetites rankled in his breast, and urged him to make some sinister exertions to gratify them. He seems to have had no relish for those violent cures for violent passions pointed out by the examples of the Sacred Fathers. Not *he,* good soul * ! *He* sought not to subdue, but to satisfy the cravings of nature; he honoured his passions, and scrupled not to make them the most costly sacrifices.

I know not whether custom or statute has imposed on our churchmen the rule of not employing

---

* It would have been carrying the mortification of the flesh *rather* too far, to plunge into a well in a cold winter's night, or to roll himself *nudior ovo* in a field of snow, like Francis and other saints of holy memory.

themselves in any handicraft, or other ostensible bodily occupation to gain money; but it is so proper
a tribute to decency, so necessary to the performance of their functions, and so correspondent to their
evangelical character, that every one must regret
when its spirit is in the slightest degree violated.
In one kind of *bodily* traffic, (usually the first in
which clergymen engage), although the world talks
loudly of their skill and address, it is certainly not
disposed to charge them with blame; and that is
the *matrimonial*. In obeying the dictates of nature, it
is no doubt a happy circumstance when *an estate*
as well as *a wife* can be obtained. It makes a com-
fortable improvement in the condition of the individual, without taking him out of the way of his
profession; and his good fortune never gives occasion to censure, when it is found to make no bad
impression on his character.

Maskwell followed this old-beaten path, and, by
a matrimonial adventure, partially realized his wishes. He found his *weight* in society much increased
by a respectable addition to his fortune; and his
power " to feast and be mellow" agreeably enlarged. It is seldom, however, that riches do not
taint the heart; and we have oftener occasion to

observe a vitiation than improvement of character in those who possess them. They are the source of many evils, and of that greatest of all evils, *the want of more*. Maskwell having got a little money into his hands, his wits were set immediately on edge to discover how it could be most profitably employed; and although fettered by a profound reverence for *the cloth*, he still found that a partner might *sleep*, and a jobber traffic in land, without much offending public observation.

The impropriety of churchmen employing themselves in any occupation foreign to that in which they have ostensibly engaged, consists greatly in its tendency to estrange them from the performance of their duty; and if that effect is produced, it is no matter in what manner, or under what cloak. A man may as well take up a trowel, as be for ever absorbed in building plans. The evil is the same, though in different shapes. It is this effect which the public charge on Maskwell. His worldly concerns have entirely engrossed his attention. His duties are in continual pursuit of him, and have oftener the fortune of missing than finding him.

This is not the full measure of the evil which has grown out of Maskwell's excessive thirst for money,—

*Perdidit arma, locum virtutis deseruit, qui*
*Semper in augenda festinat et obruitur re.*

HORACE.

His wealth has rendered him proud and imperious in his manners, inconsiderate and insolent in his language. We never turn from him with pleasure; seldom without our feelings being disgusted. Are not these faults doubly reprehensible in a minister of peace, whose labours lie so much among the meek and lowly?

Would this were all! He who is wrapt up in the desire of gain, has indeed *deserted the path of virtue;* and principle and feeling become alike banished from his breast. Let me ask Maskwell how his *filial* and *fraternal* duties stand affected by his base passion for money? Has he acted with generosity or justice in either?

" *Quidquid sub terra est, in apricum proferet ætas.*"

# DR L\*\*\*\*\*\*\*.

*The good alone have joys sincere,*
*The good alone are great.*

BEATTIE.

Amid the arid deserts of a southern sun, how refreshing is a spring of water to the thirsty traveller! how exhilerating the appearance of a palmyra, blooming in verdure, to his dejected soul! Can it be less grateful to the feelings, to turn a while from the vice and folly we have been reviewing, and to contemplate an object of genuine worth and virtue?

Although the consideration of a vicious character is the surest mean of unfolding the errors of our own, it is chiefly by the contemplation of a virtuous one, that a resolution of amendment is strengthened and confirmed. The impression is more violent in the one case, but not so lasting as in the other. The abhorrence with which we contemplate a picture of vice, is too ardent a feeling to be long indulged, and evaporates soon; but the admiration raised by a display of virtue, is a calm yet exquisite sensation, which takes a kindred and impressive hold of the mind. It beholds the picture of what it was before sullied by corruption; it feels as in its proper element; every dormant principle of right is kindled; and the impression is fondly indulged, until it assumes an influence, perhaps produces a total revolution in our habits.

The character before me presents an example of virtue, which is seldom equalled in the circle of the world. Envy itself is silent while his praise is told, or joins the general tribute of approbation and applause. In public as well as private life, his excellence is alike conspicuous; his virtue presents itself in so many amiable relations, that the eulogist finds himself at a loss upon which to fix as the most eminent and praiseworthy.

Born to an independent fortune, and blessed with superior talents, the exertions of his life have been devoted to promote the comfort and happiness of his fellow-creatures. The value of these gifts he only estimated in so far as they extended his capacity of doing good. They gave birth to no selfish pride, nor idle ambition of worldly distinction. Contentment filled his breast, and warmed it with gratitude and benevolence. He sought to diffuse the same feelings around him, to teach men to be happy, and to be grateful to the Author of their happiness.

From a firm belief in the excellence of Christianity, of its tendency to promote the present as well as future interests of mankind, he became a minister of that holy system. Actuated by the same benevolence and elevation of mind which guided him in the choice of this important profession, he despised the idea of profiting by his labours, and devoted the whole of his ecclesiastical revenue to the poor. Noble example, worthy of record and imitation! How doubly conspicuous is its merit, when we reflect on the numbers of his brethren, who, wallowing in wealth, yet greedily endeavour to increase it by every mite, which the religion they profess should teach them to bestow on the widow and the orphan!

The beneficence of the amiable L——— has not been confined to this generous sacrifice. A large part of his private fortune has been annually expended in the relief of affliction and distress. The view of misery never meets his eye, but every humane and tender principle of his nature is excited.

He has been known to take the shoes from his feet, and bestow them on the shivering mendicant, whose coverings

*————————— " had long withstood*
*" The winter's fury and encroaching frosts."*

What an interesting picture of benevolence !

*" Careless their merits, or their faults to scan,*
*" His pity gave e'er charity began."*

The beneficence of this excellent man is distinguished by that delicacy which is ever inseparable from purity of sentiment. His benefactions are bestowed with an engaging tenderness, which increases the feeling of gratitude, while it precludes the idea of obligation. They are done *in secret ;* the applause of his own breast, not that of the world, is the reward to which he aspires.

Who can behold so distinguished an example of benevolence and virtue, without a degree of sympathetic emotion? What sorrow must attend the reflection, that misfortunes have limited his power to do good, by depriving him of any part of that wealth which he administered with a fidelity so worthy the steward of his Great Master !

If we trace Dr L——— in his ministerial functions, we still find him the same elevated and upright character ; persuasive in his exhortations, watchful over the welfare of his flock ; kind and affectionate to those under affliction and sorrow. We behold an example of that respect and esteem which ministers of religion may derive from their situation. He shews, that it is not by parade, nor by punctilious acts of devotion, still less by grimace or by the intrigues of hypocrisy, that they can render themselves dear to their people, or formidable to the enemies of the faith, but by those virtues of which the hearts of the people are the judge, and which exhibit to every eye an image of that Being who is justice and beneficence itself.

In domestic life we perceive every circumstance tending to promote his happiness. All the pleasure which virtuous exertion produces he enjoys, undisturbed by any doubt of the estimation in which his motives may be held by the world. Conscious of the benevolence of his own feelings towards others, he inclines to believe that they are actuated by the like. Sensible of the imperfections of human nature, he is ever disposed to make allowance for its errors; no injury can unruffle his mind, or lessen the extent of his philanthropy.—In every domestic relation, we view him friendly, beneficent, and just. In the field of science, we are called to respect him for his erudition, and for his exertions in enlarging the bounds of knowledge. His views are liberal and comprehensive, obscured neither by bigotry nor by scepticism. He feels the benign influence of science upon human nature, and assiduously promotes the diffusion of it among mankind.

Such is the worthy L————, whose excellencies I regret the inadequacy of my pen to delineate. May he long enjoy the sweetest of all reflections; the reflection of having done good to mankind! " It forms a comfort under distress, and serves to heighten every pleasure. No affliction can take it from us, no joy can render it superfluous."

# CHRISTALIA.

*Accomplishments have taken virtue's place,*
*And wisdom falls before exterior grace.*

COUPER.

THE fair CHRISTALIA holds a conspicuous rank among the fashionables of the present day ; and merits our attention, as affording an example of the many evils which attend an ambitious desire of distinction in the gay world.

Christalia is indebted to nature for a lively disposition, and considerable powers of mind; but these advantages have been perverted and debased by a bad education. The glare of false grandeur easily captivates vulgar minds. It was the lot of Christalia's parents to be suddenly elevated from poverty to affluence. Riches engendered pride, and pride a desire of distinction. Observing the weight attached to what are termed *fashionable* accomplishments, they conceived the idea, that, to excel in these, was the only way to public estimation. They accordingly plunged into the most unlimited extravagance, and made fashion their model in every thing;—in their house and furniture, their dress, their taste, their opinions. The young Christalia escaped not the evil contagion; her attention was withdrawn from every solid pursuit, and devoted to *fashionable* attainments. The sole object of these is to regulate the external appearance; the cultivation of the mind is out of question.

> " *All that interferes and dares to clash*
> " *With ignorance and luxury, is trash.*"

Christalia swerved not from the course of education marked out to her,

> " *Till tamed and tortured into foreign graces,*
> " *She came to sport her face at public places,*
> " *And with arch-laughing eyes behind her fan,*
> " *To act her part with that great actor, man.*"

The *exterior* appearance of Christalia certainly does credit to the care which has been bestowed upon it. She possesses an agreeable expression of features, a little distorted, however, with conceit: her person is handsome, and improved by a good carriage; she dresses with elegance, is easy in her manners, possesses several useful accomplishments, and prattles with the most satisfactory gaiety. Such are the exterior qualities of Christalia. For *internal* graces, we are doomed to a fruitless search. Her mind is absorbed with vanity and ambition,—a vanity of her person, and an ambition to force it into notice. These pernicious passions never beat higher in any female breast than in that of Christalia. The ambition of shining, as a fine lady, appears to have become the paramount rule of her actions, and to have risen superior to every consideration of modesty or prudence. It has suppressed that sensibility of soul, which is the brightest ornament of a female character, and has rendered her callous to every deviation from moral rectitude.

Do I speak too severely of a passion, which is borne upon a cloud of proofs? From how great a want of feeling could Christalia behold that wealth, which gave birth to the extravagance and folly in which she has so long been bantled, driven to the winds, and *the credit* of the world repeatedly forfeited, with-

out feeling corrected and humbled! How great was
her indiscretion, in appearing, amid the ruins of a father's fortune, as gay, as splendid as ever, excelling
the daughters of every honest and *unbroken* citizen!

" —— *Heic vivimus ambitiosa*
" *Paupertate omnes."*
" *Though poor, ambitious still to shine."*

—Alas! how true is the remark of D'Alembert, that
ambition is the only passion which " has no respect
" to blood, to friendship, nor to duty."

But I may be accused of harshness, in loading the
fragile subject before me with animadversions, which
fall with more propriety on those who have placed
the viper in her bosom, and fostered it there,
by their encouragement and protection. On them,
indeed, the censure falls with tenfold force; but who
would attempt to pierce a rock to draw forth water?
Habits with old people become too inveterate to afford a prospect of eradication.

" *He who at fifty is a fool,*
" *Is far too stubborn grown for rule."*

It is not them I would endeavour to impress with a sense of the vicious folly of an idle ambition; it is the fair, misguided Christalia, in whom I trust there still remains some germ of feeling and moral sense. Let her be persuaded, that to attract the gaze of the world is a miserable compensation for its contempt and reprobation; that to gain the admiration of others, is a poor return for internal disquiet. Let her search her breast, and tell what solid pleasure or satisfaction her past pursuits have imparted to it. Then we may indulge the hope, that she will turn from the error of her ways, and follow the path of virtue and wisdom;—a path in which the natural but long suppressed energies of her mind may obtain her more lasting distinction and esteem, than ever the applause of the idle and dissolute could afford.

*So the pure limpid stream when foul with stains*
*Of rushing torrents and descending rains,*
*Works itself clear; and as it runs, refines,*
*Till by degrees the floating mirror shines;*
*Reflects each flower that on the border grows,*
*And a new heaven in its fair bosom shows.*

ADDISON.

# DR GROVEL.

---

*Alas!* ———————————————
*What mighty dulness of itself can do !*
CHURCHILL.

" *Fruges consumere nati.*"

" *For loaves and fishes born to scramble.*"

---

" To raise monkeys to men, to degrade men to monkeys; to attempt to annihilate or extenuate the line of partition between them, is a reigning taste in philosophy *." Sceptics are not content to witness the degradation of an individual below the rest of his species, and to allow him the slender stability which he acquires from standing at the bottom of the scale, but invidiously reduce him to a level with the most degraded of the whole animal world. Every

---

\* Lord Woodhouselee's Life of Kames.

person of sober judgment will be disposed to regret the existence of a spirit of generalization, which is productive of conclusions so gross and extreme.

It is however, unfortunate, that the qualities of many in society should afford too much food for this levelling spirit: and among *the many*, the subject of the present stricture holds a very conspicuous station. It has often been facetiously remarked by the celebrated Dr G******, that were he to make out a scale of the animal world, he would place MAN *at the top*, and——Dr GROVEL *at the bottom !*

This ill-regarded individual has had the *misfortune* to be elevated, by the pretension of great talents, to a situation, the lustre of which has not only exposed his defects, but rendered these doubly obnoxious by rendering them conspicuous. He presents an example of what a supple and cunning disposition, checked by no feeling of delicacy or honour, can achieve in human life; and shews, that the eminence of dignity is easier to be gained by flattering and beguiling the passions that guard it, than by obtaining the countenance of the goddess of reason, who holds the nominal control over it.

Possessed of feeble and narrow powers of mind, this Reverend Doctor has never dived farther into

literature, than the necessity of a *graduation* requi-
red: Yet he has always had enough to say of his
talents, but has wisely refrained from bringing their
excellence to a test.   He is in truth

―――――――― " *No intellectual lion,*
" *Subduing every thing he darts his eye on;*
" *Rather,* I *ween, an intellectual* flea
" *Hopping on science's broad bony back,*
" *Poking its pert proboscis of attack,*
" *Drawing a drop of blood, and fancying it a sea.*"

Grovel's manners, however, have performed what
talents ought to have done, but which his were un-
qualified to do.  By a fawning and wily mode of
conduct, by a cautious attention to opportunity, and
by a steady regard to his personal interest, he has
pushed himself forward in society, and usurped situations of honour and trust, which ought to have been
the rewards of merit and virtue.  Without learning, he
has ventured to assume the superintendence of men
of learning! Without virtue, he has pretended to ad-
minister public affairs with integrity !

These inconsistent relations between Dr Grovel
and his occupations, put me strongly in mind of a
ludicrous picture I have seen somewhere of a com-
monwealth turned topsyturvy. ·The administration
of affairs was represented as committed to an *ouran
outang;* his coadjutors were all idiots and madmen;
and every being who could boast of intellect, was
held in leading strings by this monstrous junta.

The ignorance and imbecillity of Grovel have left
deep traces of their injurious influence on his public
administration.   Never was there one more tarnish•
ed with errors, nor more ruinous to the interests
committed to his charge.   In all his views he has
been contracted and short-sighted; and has fortified
them with that common attribute of ignorant and
weak minds,—a stubborn resistance to correction.
Through good and through bad report he has carried forward his designs to completion, crushing candid and manly opposition with the iron hand of authority, or gaining the support of the scrupulous and
wavering by his artful and insinuating addresses.
For, like every one who is actuated by no settled
principle of rectitude, while he would curry to a dog
to gain its favour, he could show his teeth where he
was aware that fawning would only exasperate.

A man who makes interest the rule of his actions, is in that respect only undeviating and steady; in the rest of his conduct he is as variable and shifting as the cameleon in its colours. So the world has beheld the opinions of Grovel for ever veering about as the genial currents of influence might chance to blow upon them; aptly resembling the flickering

——— " *straw, that's whirl'd by every blast.*"

His services have been ever at the command of wealth or power; exemplifying the degrading maxim of Walpole, that *every man has his price.* In whatever direction he may have found it necessary for a time to steer, he has been always alike zealous, alike full of pretensions to *sincerity.*

This staunch and successful place-hunter has been greatly stimulated in his progress by an insatiable spirit of avarice. The prospect of a savoury morsel has been as great a lure, as the honour of coming in at the capture. Among the clerical pack he has been always distinguished for the quickness of his scent, and his skill in pursuing the game. Not a cur among them all but could tell some instance of his superior cunning and sagacity; of the bye-roads which he has taken; of the fences he has leaped; or of the quagmires through which he has dashed, in order to outstrip his associates, and seize *the brush.* Not a Nimrod under whom he has sped the field, but could describe the fawning and insinuating manner with which, at the close of the day, he has licked his feet, or climbed his knees,

——— " *the envied crumb to snatch.*"

When the days of a man are drawing to a close, can there be a more interesting or more affecting contemplation, than to revert to the actions of his past life? How gratefully does the remembrance of good deeds refresh the mind, and sooth the cares of age! What an exhilerating light does it cast on the gloom of futurity!

*Our own strict judges, our past life we scan,*
*And ask if virtue has enlarged the span;*
*If bright the prospect, we the grave defy,*
*Trust future ages, and contented die.*

TICKELL.

In proportion as these considerations have weight on the mind, how much ought that man to suffer, who, retracing his journey through life, cannot discover one action honourable or praiseworthy; nothing upon which to rest for relief or consolation!

*A self-desci ter, from himself he strays*
*—— in vain; companions black as night,*
*His pressing cares arrest him in his flight.*

FRANCIS'S HORACE.

# DR ALAMODE.

---

" *Vel natura levat, vel medicina necat.*"

" *Some people die of old age, some of the Doctor.*"

---

Among the many arguments that have been devised against the utility of the Art of Medicine, this has been perhaps one of the most ingenious,— that notwithstanding all the discoveries and improvements which have been made in it since the days of Esculapius, as many people die now, as died then, in proportion to the different degrees of population of the earth. Fontenelle advances this argument in one of his Dialogues of the Dead ; and it will not be considered as refuted by what he asserts in reply, that physicians at least prolong our lives for a short time; since equal authorities might be cited, and much better grounds of probability be shown, to prove that as many die in an early age at the present time, as died at the same age two thousand years ago.

Now if all this be true,—if our lives not only cannot be preserved to old age, but not even prolonged for an hour, by any human means, it will follow that there is in reality no use at all in the science of medicine. A strange dilemma! which I might increase, were I to descend into a greater detail, and show, that, though the application of this science cannot serve any good purpose, the misapplication of it, by ignorant men, may serve a very bad one,—that of shortening the life which it attempts to prolong. Sure I am, it would not be hard to prove, that most people die where there is the greatest number of physicians.—But I apprehend growing too prolix ; and it is sufficient for my present purpose to inquire, What then is the true use of these gentlemen? and in what respects do they benefit the world, on which they impose? The answer is expressed by an old French epigram I have read somewhere :

" *Respectables enfans du celebre Hippocrate,*
" *Dont l'eloquent babil nous console et nous flatte.*"

They sooth and console us in sickness, and flatter us into better hopes and better spirits.

E

This end, if such they will allow me to call it, is attained by no one in a higher degree than by Dr ALAMODE. *He*, at least, appears convinced of the truth of the previous considerations, and acts accordingly ; without assuming, as is assumed every day, by men of less talents, the absurd power of preserving life. It is sufficient for him that he renders life agreeable, or, at least, *tolerable* to his patients: He presumes no farther ; for he knows the extent of human powers and human knowledge, and reveres the unalterable laws by which our constitution is governed.

Will it be said, in censure of the prudence of Dr Alamode, that he is thus apparently wise, from a real want of ability ?—That he stops thus short in the pursuit of knowledge, because nature has not gifted him, in common with other men, with the means of proceeding farther? It will be said, —it has been said,—by those persons only who wander, under the guidance of imagination, from the precincts of real, in search of fantastical and unattainable knowledge. These assume, and impose their assumptions on a silly world ; with the more success too, very often, the less they deserve it : and, to give a fair colour to their own conduct, they affect to treat the diffidence of my friend Dr Alamode as ignorance. Absurd vanity! They think it not too much for themselves to claim a knowledge and powers, to which they are incapable, by their nature, of attaining; and they bestow on Dr Alamode such a limited portion of each, as might almost degrade him from the same class of intelligent beings!

It is not without reason, therefore, that I have taken this opportunity of clearing the Doctor's character, which such persons have designedly too much abused, by doubting, or pretending to doubt, of his merits as a physician. They have indeed asked to be shown the cures he has performed; and have triumphed with a loud laugh, or a silent sneer, when no such proofs of merit could be produced. But I have shown, that *to cure* was not his object, as it ought not to be the object of others; and it would be quite as easy to demonstrate, that he has attained the *real object* which he sought to attain,—to sooth, to flatter, and to console us in pain, in sickness, and confinement. Almost every lady in ———— could furnish me with some pretty compliment of the Doctor's to relate. " Ma chere Madame! permettez-moi—'tis only to feel your pulse.——Que vous etes charmante, dans ce joli deshabille! Ah, Madame! be assured the paleurs of sickness will never over-come the bloom of that complexion.——You took the draught last night? Eh bien, Well, be so good as take another to-day, and you shall be allowed to play two hours at cards to-night." All this, I know, may be turned into ridicule; and what is there that may not? But surely it is better than the unbend-ing austerity of Dr ———, the silly airs of conse-quence of Dr ———, or, which is still worse, the harsh unfeeling manner of Dr ———. They have all gone nearly the same journey by different paths; and Dr Alamode has chosen the easiest and the shortest.

The other charges which have been brought against the Doctor's character, are equally ill-founded. It has been urged, to instance one of these, that his dress and manners are affectedly in the French taste; and are improper therefore in him, as an old man, and as a physician. To this objection we may reply by asking, Are not the French the politest nation in Europe? None will be found to deny it. And if they are so, in what respect does Dr Alamode err, in imitating those, whose study it is to be polite and complaisant? Candid men will consider it only as one great mean of attaining that object which he has proposed to himself; and it would be improper in me to descend, for the sake of the ignorant or the prejudiced, to prove it by any farther details, and lengthen a subject which I have dwelt too long upon already.

Let it suffice to say, in general, that these various objections, and others of the like nature, against Dr Alamode, will have influence on such only as are prejudiced in favour of living, and are vain enough of human nature to imagine, that human means are capable of preserving life ; but will have none with such as are content to trust in Providence, and not in men formed every way as weak and erring as themselves ; who are content to receive amusement where they cannot obtain assistance ; and to be ignorant, in order not to be imposed upon.

# MR COLUMN.

*His genius, without thought or lecture,*
*Was hugely turned to architecture.*

SWIFT.

Distinguished as the inhabitants of the city of —————— have for a long time been, for their opulence and their public spirit, it affords considerable matter of surprise, that they have been able to boast of few architects who have attained even to mediocrity of merit, and of none that have surpassed it. Even in present times, which panegyrists hold forth as so greatly advanced in point of improvement, there seems a wonderful disposition to bestow patronage upon persons absolutely devoid of every quality necessary to form a good artist. The general style of building amply confirms these observations; a meanness and vulgarity of manner being the almost invariable characteristic.

Amid such sterility of genius, it is grateful to re-
cognise a partial blaze of it in the subject now before me. The abilities of Mr Column place him
high in the local scale of his profession ; and had
not these been too much counteracted by his way-
ward propensities, they might have raised him to
very distinguished eminence. To a delicate taste he,
adds an original and creative fancy, the two greatest
characteristics of an able artist. But, from a facili-
ty of temper and a disposition to social pleasures,
which are almost become the proverbial concomi-
tants of genius, his exertions have never been properly directed to the improvement of his talents :
his studies have been the excursive whim of an hour,
suspended at the call of friendship, and renewed on
the tide of recollection and repentance. His defi-
ciencies are of course great, and the task of amendment still remains a burden on his riper years.

The architectural productions of Mr Column,
however, rank far above those of his provincial con-
temporaries. In these we observe some approach to
greatness of manner, but in those of his rivals an ab-
solute departure from it. I fear much it will be long
before a just taste in this fascinating art of architecture will be introduced among us. Are we never to

be persuaded that a multiplicity of minute ornaments, a vast variety of angles and cavities, clusters
of little columns, ranges of urns, and a multitude of
windows, are the indubitable signs of a meanness
and vulgarity of taste? Are we doomed to perpetu-
ate the barbarism of Gothic times, and never to re-
vive the pure manner of the Grecian school, in which
every decoration arises from necessity and use, e-
very pillar has something to support?

" *O Fortunati quorum* pia tecta *resurgunt,*
" *Æneas ait, et fastigia suspicit urbis.*"

Simplicity is justly esteemed a supreme excellence
in all the performances of art; as the productions of
nature are accounted of a nobler and higher order,
in proportion to their display of this quality. Let
me hope that the reign of vulgarity is not to last
for ever; and, to use the language of a Roman
Poet,

——— " *ut omnium*
" *Versabitur urna, serius, ocyus.*"

Mr Column is entitled to the gratitude of his fellow-citizens for having contributed, in some degree, to improve their taste ; and it is much to be regretted, that his careless habits should expose him to any diminution of the public favour.

# GIL SPRUCE.

---

*And I beheld among the simple ones, a young man*
*   void of understanding.*

PROVERBS.

*You silly scribbling Beau,*
*What demon made you write?*
*I'm sure to write you know*
*As much as you can fight.*

SWIFT.

---

OUR reason, of which we are so proud, has now so little, and our passions so much influence, in directing the conduct of our lives, that the question may be asked very properly, which was put by an eloquent writer of the last age, upon a different occasion: Would it not be better to walk upon four legs, to wear a long tail, and to be called a beast, with the advantage of being determined by unerring instinct to those truths that are necessary to our well-being; rather than to walk on two legs, to wear no tail, and to be honoured with the title of man, at the expence of deviating from them perpetually? Brutes are directed by instinct according to the purposes for which it was implanted in them: a bear will not attempt to fly, nor a foundered horse to leap a five-barred gate, to use expressions of Swift; but man, who is directed by reason, and by instinct too, is hurried round continually in a vortex of folly and error.

Those who consider these reasons may not be surprised, that some men, in the present age especially, have been induced to wish they had indeed been born beasts; and if they read what follows, they also may see much reason for wishing, that some particular persons had been born beasts, who act and think little becoming their stations and their duties as men. Had Mr GIL SPRUCE,, the young gentleman whose character I sketch, been born *a cock* or *a bull*, for instance, it is certain he would never have risen to that conspicuous ridicule, which he has now provoked, by attempting to write. Or had he, to descend a little, been born *really and bodily* an ass, he might have been kicked and caned, no doubt, but, it is certain it would not have been for his vanity nor his impertinence. He would have been retained and guided in the path in which he was placed by nature, without the means of becoming ridiculous, or, which is worse, of becoming odious and despicable. He would not, it is true, have travelled nor seen, as *he thinks he has seen,* the world; he would not have learned languages, nor have been a fine gentleman; *fop* is the term I would use: he would not, to be sure, either as a cock, or a bull, or an ass, have sung Italian; in fine, he would not have been in love with D———, and twenty more at the same time,—the silly character of a male coquette, to say no worse. But, on the other side, he would not have then attempted to write a book,—a great advantage surely; as the affirmative draws along with it a chain of consequences very hurtful to the character of Mr Spruce as a *human* being.

By writing, Mr Spruce intended to display, no doubt, some such advantages as those I have mentioned, as well as to display the faults and disadvantages of other people; but he did not foresee the conclusions which were drawn afterwards from the former; nor sufficiently, if at all, attend to those consequences which resulted from the latter; though both the one and the other would have been obvious enough to persons of very ordinary understanding. It was not foreseen, for instance, that from the display of those qualities by which he had chosen to describe himself, the public would conclude he was a vain, affected fool; nor that from the bold confession of vices, which he meant to be characteristic of a man of fashion, they would conclude that he either asserted most impudent falsehoods, or else that he was a base seducer, and a mean and an infamous boaster of being so.——

*Good heavens ! that sots and knaves should be so vain,*
*To wish their vile remembrance may remain ;*
*And stand recorded at their own request,*
*To future days a libel or a jest.*

DRYDEN.

Again, as to the consequences, Mr Spruce considered very little then, though he may now, perhaps, be convinced, that his extreme readiness to oblige the world with *characters*, with those of others, and with part of his own, might lead it to a fuller knowledge of the latter, than even *he* would be willing it should become possessed of. It led, as one instance

out of many I could adduce, to the discovery, that
he was an *arrant coward.*——

" *His pride regrets it ever should be said,*
" *His heels eclipsed the honours of his head.*"

Let the reader now weigh these observations, and
endeavour to determine the relative merits of *a
cock* or *a bull*, and those of Mr Gil Spruce. He
may then discover, that the notions concerning
the inferiority of powers in beasts, as well as their
degraded rank in the natural economy, in some cases,
have little foundation in fact or reason, but have
been assumed rather through the pride and vanity
of the human heart.——

" *That instinct is a surer guide*
" *Than reason, boasting mortals pride ;*
" *And that brute beasts are far before 'em,*
" Deus est anima brutorum."

He will perhaps be satisfied that a cock and a bull,
which perform the parts allotted to them in the system of nature, are preferable animals to men who
do not perform their parts at all, but act quite con-

trary to them in some points; and he may find reason indeed to exclaim, " *How unfortunate it is that
Mr Gil Spruce was not born a cock or a bull !*"

The *contemporary authority* on which I rest for
the truth of the features of this character, contains
*so just and so fine* a picture of the young man, that
I cannot conclude the subject better than by quo-
ting it.  He is, says this *elegant satyrist,* " like
a brainless youth, who, transplanted from the *bleak
regions* of ignorance, and placed by some frolic of
fortune in the *gay sunny vale* of good company, expresses his increased impertinence by *empty buzzing,*
passes the bounds which conscious inferiority had
once imposed, and overwhelms in a tide of impu-
dence and affectation, all merit, modesty, and common sense."

# MRS SANDY.

*Si un tel objet entroit avec tous ces grands noms,*
*Le sourcil rehaussé d'orgueilleuses chimeres,*
*Je lui diroit bientot : Je connois tous vos pères.*

BOILEAU.

" *Should such as she approach me with this vanity,*
" *This overbearing pride in all her looks,*
" *I'd tell her of her ancestors.*"

IT was one of the precepts of Hamlet to the play-
ers, to " suit the action to the word, the word to the
action." The rule may be extended into a principle
of conduct in life, founded on the justest reason, and
extremely applicable to many who tread the stage
at present ; who act on no other principle, but to
gratify a reigning passion, or to follow a prevailing
mode. It may teach us to suit our manner of living
to the sphere in which we live, and that sphere to
our means,—a lesson too much neglected by such
as I have alluded to.

These persons continue steady in a mode of conduct which most of them have had reason to desire
they had never pursued; and act on principles, which
not one of them, I will venture to say, would dare to
avow without a blush. It becomes more necessary
to teach this lesson, as the difficulty of practising it
increases, and to enforce it by such means as lie in
our power, that vice may be discouraged and its
mischievous influence be checked. This is no chi-
merical, but a real duty ; and were it discharged as
it ought to be, in every case, or at least as it might
be, in many, we should see fewer of those persons
affect the airs and the vices of people of rank,
who were born, perhaps, *to a washing-tub:* we should
see fewer Halfworths and Sandys among us. But
if this vice be so great in itself, (and I could bring
many more examples of it than the subject of this
stricture), what will be the feelings of every honest
breast, when it is beheld both heightened by an overbearing pride, that affects the highest state, and debased, if I may say so, by a disgusting meanness,
that descends to the lowest? Strong indignation will
be one feeling, and profound contempt another. Mrs
Sandy merits both. Born in a low sphere of life,
in one no higher than that which I have just now

supposed, and possessed of no talents to fit her for a
better, it might be thought she would have been
modest, (not from principle, but prudence), upon her
elevation from this situation, the better to conceal
her defects, which prosperity tended rather to display. It was so thought at the time; but a contrary
line of conduct which she pursued, soon excited those
feelings of indignation and contempt in the breasts
of her fellow-citizens, and have forced upon me the
unpleasant task of displaying to the world the vices
and follies of a person whom I would have wish-
ed rather to have passed over in silence. Yet when
we see a woman abuse the advantages which fortune
has given her; to arrogate others, such as merit alone
can give; and assert, and support her claims to these
advantages, by a conduct contrary to the principles
from which merit arises; when we see her act inde-
cently, considering the former sphere of her life, and
absurdly, considering the present; in a word, when we
see her both retain the vulgarity and meanness of low
life, and assume all the pride and silly vanity of rank,
without balancing either, by bringing any virtue from
the former, or by using the latter to any good purpose,
—it is hard to refrain from the strongest expressions
of reprobation. When the cause of virtue is concerned,

the meanest hand may interpose in its defence ; and I am too sensible of the power of example, not to fear danger even from Mrs Sandy.

I hold up the picture, therefore, as a mirror to the ladies, wherein many may behold their own folly at full length, and in so contemptible a light, that the deformity may recall them, if possible, to reason and virtue. Should these consequences ensue, and I do not altogether despair of so desireable a change among the ladies of ——, we may behold, without much regret, Mrs Sandy as vulgar and ill bred as the means she has had of being so can render her, and much more extravagant than her fortune can permit her to be : we may then, perhaps, without regret, behold her,

—————————————— " *flutter on,*

" *From toy to toy, from vanity to vice ;*

" *Till, blown away by death, oblivion come*

" *Behind, and strike her from the book of life.*"

THOMSON.

# SQUIRE CHATTERMORE.

---

*His wits were sent him for a token,*
*But in the carriage crack't and broken.*

BUTLER.

---

IT will readily be allowed, that every man ought
to rest for estimation upon his own personal merit,
and that nothing is more contemptible than the pride
of descent

> *Let your own acts immortalize your name,*
> *'Tis poor relying on another's fame ;*
> *For, take the pillars but away, and all*
> *The superstructure must to ruins fall.*

DRYDEN'S JUV.

It is a frailty, however, which few have the hardy
virtue to correct, to bring forward the qualities of
their ancestors for admiration ;—a fondness infla-

med by the hope, that in admiring the blaze of the comet, the tail will not pass without some share of distinction. However little I may be disposed to respect such a propensity, I would blame myself for taking any thing away from this unworthy subject, by suppressing circumstances to which his pride has formed a strong attachment; and my readers will therefore pardon my recurring to the past, while endeavouring to sketch the follies of the present.

Know then, all ye who have not steeled your souls against the indulgence of admiration, that the noted Squire CHATTERMORE traces his descent to one of the most distinguished philosophers of a recent age, who generated the connection

—— *" In the lusty stealth of nature."*

Know, that the genius of this great man passed in undiminished vigour to his immediate offspring, and was exerted by them in a manner not less transcendant, perhaps still more romantic. As that eminent philosopher endeavoured to explode all former systems of the universe as erroneous, and to establish a more reasonable one of his own invention, so we have found his offspring actuated by the same sublime spirit, soaring beyond the contracted limits of human ingenuity, and astonishing the world with un-imagined discoveries. People still look back with wonder on the Archimedean attempt of one of the Squire's progenitors, to make coaches roll over hill and dale *without e'er a horse to draw them!* and still complain of the blind cupidity of those in authority, who could discourage so noble an invention, from the paltry consideration that it would diminish the *post-horse duty,* or be prejudicial to the interests of *horse jockies.*— Some may smile at the recollection of —— *hill;* but did they know the vile nefarious means which were used by those inimical to the important discovery, to produce the unfortunate, the ludicrous stoppage of the carriage *at the bottom,* they would call back rigidity to their muscles, and shed tears on the degeneracy of the times, and the misfortunes of genius.

Enough of so dolorous a subject!—It is time to turn to the individual before us, who boasts of his descent from this great, but unfortunate mechanist. The Squire has, fortunately for himself, inherited little of that extravagance of imagination which distinguished his forefathers. In his quickness of perception, volatility of spirits, and weakness of judgment, we may still, however, discover some blazing embers of the spirit of the illustrious Chattermores. Convinced by sad example of the inefficacy of literary acquirements to procure either comfort or independence, this hopeful youth spent not his days in dissecting triangles or tetragonals, or in investigating the powers of mechanism. He contented himself with pursuing a more humble path in the world; and skimmed the surface of knowledge for its more showy and ornamental advantages only. He gleaned superficial information, and searched deeply into no subject;—a habit which has given him the quality of speaking tolerably on all things, although he is intimately acquainted with none. The polite arts have been an object of the Squire's peculiar regard, and he has cultivated them with considerable success. Let me select a few instances:—The Squire can sketch scenery,—he can tune a flageolet,—he can dance with ease,—and, moreover, in all these accomplishments, he *humbly* apprehends himself to be a *virtuoso*. On the merits of a Rembrandt, a Haydn, or a Parker, he will discourse with the nicest discrimination, and tell to a degree how much this excelled in colouring, that in execution, the other in attitude!

These varied and *valuable* qualities have rendered Chattermore a being of no mean consequence in the drawing-room. But he has the misfortune of pleasing only the silly gossipers of that circle, and no others. His manners are offensive and disgusting to men of sense. The volubility of his utterance, his pert flippancy embracing a great deal of the *concisum ac minutum* of Tully, and his everlasting garrulity, never fail to set the feelings of his auditors on edge. However trifling the subject may be, the Squire is always right vehement in his speech ; but instead of producing a consonant impression on others, the effect is usually a ludicrous exposure of his own weakness and absurdity. His head is perpetually swimming in a flood of self-sufficiency ; and he has the appearance of never going beyond his depth. On every thing, however great his ignorance may be, he appears always quite *at home*, and as one who could learn nothing *new*. Society imposes no restraint, but rather gives a spur to his licentious freedom. He seems to think all around him so silly or ignorant, that they ought to say nothing ; and himself so able and well informed, that every one else ought to listen to his perpetual talk. The privilege of exclusively jabbering for *an hour* is indeed a great one; but Chattermore seems to have formed no idea of *any* limits to his usurpation. To get rid of this truly insufferable *bore,* his friends have only one alternative, that is, either by flying off as quick as they can; before their *membrana tympani* are altogether deafened, or by forcing the busy magpie to make his exit in some genteel and not *unfashionable* manner.

The Squire's heart boasts of as little as his head. He is of a mean disingenuous disposition, which leads him to the vilest means to promote any object he has in view. But let me draw a veil over the scene which here opens to view; for the greatest stretch of imagination will be infinitely more merciful to Chattermore than a disclosure of the reality. ————

\* \* \* \* \* \* \* \* \*
\* \* \* \* \* \* \* \* \*
\* \* \* \* \*

# SIMON GRIPEALL.

*O esecrabile avarizia ! O ingorda*
*Fame d'avere !————*

ARIOSTO.

" *Curst avarice ! insatiate thirst of gain !*"

THERE is scarce any vice or folly more ridiculous
among the sons of men, and there are few, therefore,
which have been more exclaimed against in all ages,
than an immoderate love of wealth. The subject may
now be well considered as exhausted ; and I may be
censured for treating of a matter that has been treated
already, in the writings of so many great men, though
with little effect upon society. Seneca shall excuse
me. He says, in one of his epistles, that men trust
more readily to their eyes, than to their ears ; that
the way by precept is long, by example short and ef-
fectual. " Homines amplius oculis quam auribus

credunt; longum iter est per precepta, breve et effi-
cax per exempla." This judgment is founded on observation of the passions of mankind. Example
speaks to these, flatters them, and animates them
on the side of virtue, or deters them from vice. It
assuages them likewise, and allows judgment to enter into the cause. In a word, the moral character
is thus formed, and a right turn given to our ways of
thinking, more effectually, and more permanently,
than by the finest system of philosophy, or the most
splendid eloquence. Declamation on this subject
would be, as Hamlet expresses it,

" *Weary, stale, flat, and unprofitable;*"

but personify the vice by examples which we all
know, and know therefore to be true, it then comes
home to our minds and bosoms, to use an expression
of my Lord Bacon; the lesson is made in some sort
practical, and we receive instruction from fact, when
we might disbelieve speculation.

To apply to my present purpose the general reflection, let us turn our eyes on Mr GRIPEALL. In
him we shall see the vice of avarice in all its deformity : we shall see it in its strength, and in its conse-

quences: we shall see it despicable in itself, and hurtful to society. And no man will behold it, in such colours as those, without feelings of contempt and detestation.

Every mean vice that is incident to human nature, is allied very nearly to the love of wealth,—extreme ignorance, a total contempt of virtue, a disregard of fame, a perversion of all that is good in us, and an application of all that is bad, to a base end. These form conspicuous features in the character of Mr Gripeall. But they are not all. The example shows a great deal more. It shews farther, that sentiments of a much higher rank may enter into the composition of such a character. Religion has entered largely into that of Mr Gripeall. But this proper mistress of human life and knowledge, whose office it is to conduct us rightly in both, becomes in him degraded to a vile superstition, the child of ignorance and fear: she is reduced to connive at the indulgence of passions, and to be the cloak of principles and actions, the correction of which is one of her greatest objects. She has taught him neither charity nor mercy, nor good will towards men; she has rendered his mind gloomy and contracted like his heart, in proportion as he affected more, or really *sought* more perhaps to honour and obey her. Yet this very earnestness of zeal carries with it an advantage to Mr Gripeall,—the advantage of being better enabled, as he shows more sincerity, to impose his knaveries and follies on a credulous world. This he has done ; and both in society, and the church, from the weight of his purse in the one, and his zeal in the other, he has carried higher his pretensions to public eminence, the less pretensions he has had to the public esteem.

# A GROUPE,

─────────

*Petits papillons d'un moment,*
*Invisibles marionettes,*
*Qui volez si rapidement,*
*Du Polichinelle au neant.*

VOLTAIRE.

" *Ye sunshine butterflies,*
" *Poor puppets of a day,*
" *To Punches rank who rise,*
" *Are laughed at, and decay.*"

─────────

THEATRES, ever since they were invented, having been compared very aptly to the world; and the world in return having been compared as aptly to a theatre; I may be permitted to descend a little, and compare some societies, such as the one I propose to describe, to a Puppet-show.

Besides the many and manifest advantages that puppet-shows possess in general, which I shall not stop to enumerate, there is this farther advantage in the show I mean to exhibit, that the amusement we receive from it may tend to make us both better and wiser ; for my puppets do not move like others on springs of wire, but on those that move by far the greater part of mankind,—the springs of knavery, folly, passion, and whim.

    *" Come then the colours and the ground prepare ;"*

let the curtain be raised.

— · —

    Behold Beau FRIBBLE, Ladies and Gentlemen, who very naturally, as naturally as it is for ignorance to be presumptuous, pushes first upon the stage. This nature's nothing, this " thing of things," as Swift says, produced under a sun that ripened soon the weeds of folly in his mind, (an easy matter where there was no judgment to check their growth), and spoiled even *in his formation,* was sent nevertheless to this stage, that he might be the better displayed ;—acted for a little time the part of a fool, and then attempting the character of a fine gentleman, fell, from a love of his native country, I suppose, into that of an ape. In this shape I have presumed to exhibit him—acting like an ape, grinning and prating like an ape, and biting also like an ape: an ape in every thing but understanding;—there, to do justice to the apes, I must confess my puppet is infinitely below them.

―――――

" Oh tempora, Oh mores! hem! Cicero."—This, Ladies and Gentlemen, is Dr QUOTEM, something like a statue, as Pope says,

" *Stepp'd from its pedestal to take the air;*"

a learned puppet, who has crowded as much into his head, as could be crowded into any block head whatever. His learning has only this fault; it is of no use to any one, to himself least of all ; but may be, as it often is, extremely troublesome to others. " Facheuse suffisance qu'une suffisance purement livresque," says Montaigne, very justly ; or, in the decent language of our time, " What a horrible bore book impertinence is!" Dr Quotem, placed in this age of the world, is very much like a Dutch traveller in a foreign country, who gapes and stares indiscriminately at every thing, without understanding any thing. Ask him a question about the events that passed two thousand years ago, and you wind up the spring that sets all the machine a-going: it then rattles on with vast rapidity, and confused noise, until its force is spent, but not until you are stunned and stupified. Speak to him, on the contrary, of such events as have happened in later times, such as relate to the interest and wellbeing of his own country: he becomes then as mute a puppet as ever was formed of wood. " Dieu le fasse donc la grace de devenir moins savant;"—a wish I have read somewhere or other, and which I translate, that all may join with me in it,—" *The Lord be charitable to him, and make him less learned.*"

————

" John Gilpin *was a citizen,*
" *Of credit and renown,*
" *A train band captain eke was he;*
" *In famous* ——— *town.*"

Here, Ladies and Gentlemen, is a true patriot—in wood,

I mean; one who wears a sword in defence of his liberties, and for his country is ready, at all times, to lay down his—*ell-measure!* For their sakes, he fears no danger, and refuses no fatigue : he submits to reviews, and marches, and countermarches; he endures rain, and wind, and cold ; and now minds the firing of gunpowder no more than the bite of a flea.

" *Dulce et decorum est pro patriâ militare.*"

Moulded from true heart of oak himself, and acting upon the springs of honesty and plain sense, he comprehends little of those patriots of rotten wood, who are *patriots* till they get in, and then are——— *ministers* till they're turned out.

———————

Permit me now to introduce to your notice, Miss DEBORAH PRIM, one of those

"*Thoughtful beings, long and spare,*"

called in the language of the world, Old Maids.

Philosophers have disputed much about the use of this species of beings, but it is now generally allowed that they tread the stage of this life as beacons only to all young ladies that are sailing to the harbour of Matrimony. Miss Deborah, to carry on the metaphor, is a beacon set upon the rock Pride, as others are upon the quicksands of Vanity; and appears with this sour, sullen, gloomy aspect, merely to intimate to all such as approach, that they will remain wind bound for ever after on the shores of Ill-nature and Deformity. I cannot lengthen the detail of Miss Prim's qualities, for she has only two springs to go upon, Old Age and Ugliness; which when pressed cause her to emit a *disagreeable noise*, resembling the grating of a door on rusty hinges. At all other times, she lives peaceably enough with the two emblems of herself,—her parrot, and her cat; ignorant of the supreme, unclouded, eternal joys of a married life!

---

Ha! here he comes. — This, Ladies and Gentlemen, I assure you, whatever you may think, is the *handsomest* puppet in Britain, *were it not for his d—d legs.* " What!" you cry,

———————————————— " *that thing of silk?*

" *C —— that mere white curd of asses milk ?*"

Yes indeed.—He has got a paper head to be sure,
but that only shows there may be paper skulls as well
as wooden brains.  But, in return, consider he's a
soldier.—No!

    " *Not a soldier at all, but an officer I,*
    " *A col'nel who carries a sword on his thigh.*"

Hear how he talks! A valuable puppet!—*Were it not
for his d—d legs.*  No piece of wood here possesses
more advantages than he does.

    " *A brain of feathers, and a heart of lead,*"

and a light pair of heels too, to suit occasion.  He
moves upon the springs, first, of vanity, secondly, of
vanity, thirdly, of vanity ; so that the spring being
threefold, and likewise unique, it carries him higher
in the air, and sinks him lower in the dirt, than ever
a Harlequin went before.  In short, and to draw a
conclusion, (a difficult matter, in this case), he holds
out to the world a very strong proof, that,

" *Your Omurs, and Novads, and Bluturks, and stuff,*
" *By G—d they don't signify this pinch of snuff;*
" *To give a young gentleman right education,*
" *The army's the only good school in the nation.*"

———————

The next I shall exhibit is a puppet who *would
be a Merchant,* and is always to be seen, therefore,
with a busy bustling air, and a face of deep concern.
Though it is easy to conceive there cannot be much
in a wooden head, yet observe him running continually about as if his fortune was depending on his a-
gility, or rather as if a bailiff was behind him. Now
you see him stop suddenly, like a man perplexed
and deliberating ; now, with the fore finger of his
right hand on the thumb of his left, apparently cal-
culating how much the profits of a cargo would be,
—*if it was his;* and again,

" *Knocking his pate, to see if wit will come—*
" *Alas ! in vain—there's nobody at home.*"

I confess I hesitate in ascribing ambition to be
the spring of all this ridiculous importance ; yet so

it is. This person, with just as little ability as any puppet can have, aspires nevertheless to consequence and distinction. There are many such on the stage of the world,—men who can see in themselves a merit which no other can,

—————————— " *And thus feel a pride,*
" *In seeing more than all the world beside;*"

while every part of their conduct implies a total absence of common sense.

————————

Who's he? Is that your Clown?—That! that grave, demure looking fellow? No, that man is married. To be sure he was once our fool, and used to be remarkably at home *in riding with his face to the horse's tail,* playing tricks *with blue stockings, &c.* But then he got married to a *Wax Doll,* and immediately after that, you know, lost all his suppleness. He is now only a stalking horse for his wife to ———— Hush! here are more ladies, and it would be encroaching on their prerogative to talk scandal.

———

This, Ladies and Gentlemen, is Miss RATTLE, and this Miss TATTLE, and this Mr TIPPET,—all puppets of fashion; that is, people who do less and talk more than any other body; who have the privilege of retailing scandal, and inventing it too, without restriction; at whose

     " *Every word a reputation dies ;*"

and, when tired of that amusement, to whom

     " *Snuff or the fan supply each pause of chat,*
     " *With laughing, singing, ogling, and all that.*"

An agreeable life!——These puppets, Ladies and Gentlemen, are of a singular construction, being quite hollow in the heart, which renders them very light and easy when they are about any dirty action, such as stabbing a character; and makes Mr TIPPET very agile likewise, when he is dancing to the tune of a cane; —a tune, by the way, which he is very apt to dance to, unless the spring of his heart is pressed, and his

" spirits sent down to the muscles of his knees, which are instantly ready to perform their motion, by taking up the legs with incomparable celerity, in order to remove the body out of harm's way *." In the hollow space within these puppets, there are a thousand little beings that float up and down, called Whims, Vanities, Follies, Jealousies, Piques, Quarrels, Desires, New Dresses, &c.

" *Multaque præterea magnum per inane vagantur,*"

and act as springs to keep the body in perpetual motion. To give you a history of these, would be to give you the history of a fashionable lady's life, and that is as much above my power, as beyond my comprehension.

---

* Descartes' Treatise on the Passions. Part iii.

———

I proceed, therefore, to exhibit to you Mr BOBBY DOWNWARDS, so called from his peculiar excellence in making a bow. This arises from his being very empty and light from the heels upwards, and having a head with an unusual quantity of lead in it; so that the latter, gravitating with peculiar force from its immense weight towards the earth, he is never in an erect position, but bending down, as if he was seeking something in the dirt among his feet. This puppet, Ladies and Gentlemen, is possessed of the almost incredible power of writing *satires and sonnets,* of which I have an excellent collection *at the low price of twopence each.* But, before proceeding, I must beg your pardons for having so many of my puppets,—puppies. It arises, I believe, from the great affinity there is between a wooden head and a puppy's head; and as the world,—the ladies in particular, encourage the puppies so much, I have been obliged, in deference to them, to bring these so often upon the stage. I must likewise entreat your pardons for bringing before you a puppet of so little importance,—one who acts no higher a part here, than any little *attorney's clerk* does on the great theatre of the world. I own the fault. It is, as Pope says, like breaking a butterfly upon a wheel. But I own, too, that I desired very much to display before you

" *This painted child of dirt, that stinks and stings ;*
" *Whose buz the witty and the fair annoys ;*"

that you may see in him the wonderful faculty of writing verses, never seen in any piece of wood before. This faculty is produced by three springs, vanity, impertinence, and dulness, operating at once upon his heart, and causing a paralytic motion in it, which forces open its valves, and ejects from it a liquor like froth through the greater Carotid artery up to the head, with excessive rapidity. This liquor running through the masses of lead, deposited in his skull, as I mentioned before, extracts from them the venom called Acetite, with which having incorporated, they soon after burst out together from his finger ends, under the likeness of ink; assuming, according to the quantity of the aforesaid venom, the figures of sonnets, satires, conundrums, or witty sayings.

To prove the possession of this wonderful power, he shall now sing you a song of his own composing; and with it I beg leave to close my exhibition for this time; with the design, however, of returning to open it soon, with many more puppets that are already made, besides some that are forming.

## BOBBY,

### A BALLAD *.

On Mount Parnassus long I gazed
   With pangs of hunger torn;
At length, in night's wild dreary maze
   I crept up quite forlorn.——

  " Oh thin, thin are my breeches now,
   And cold, cold blaws the win',
My purse is low, and living dear—
   Ye muses, let me in."——

  " What caitiff knocks at our castle gate ?
   Who makes so loud a din ?——

---

* For an impudent parody on this *beautiful little ballad*, see the Edinburgh Magazine for March 1809.

Go, young man, go, you need not wait,
    For here you can't get in."


" O do ye then reject that voice,
    Ye might by this time know?
Do ye reject poor Bobby's voice,
    Nor will ye hear his woe!"


" Bobby, is't you! you impudent,
    Vile scribe, our greatest *shame!*
You need not think to enter here,
    So if you please, *begone* *."


" Oh if ye wont as muses feel,
    Yet, yet as women do!
For colder blows the winter win'
    And colder I grow too."—


" At the foot of our hill there is a ditch
    Prepared for each bad poet;

---

* This poet, it is necessary to observe, never sacrifices sense to sound, and therefore commits now and then a trifling inaccuracy of rhyme, in order the better to preserve the entire beauty of the verse.

There go !—We need not tell the way,
For you by this time know it."


" And must I then!—why then I must,—
Ladies, your will be done !
There will I go, and starve and fret,
And scribble, scribble on."


### FINIS.

Lightning Source UK Ltd.
Milton Keynes UK
UKHW020308261118
332889UK00007B/244/P